# Self-Care Moments
## A Workbook to Navigate Your Grief

Krista Helman, MSW

FernAura Press
Ottawa, ON

Publisher - FernAura Press

101-2039 Robertson Road

Ottawa, Ontario, K2M 1P2



*Self-Care Moments: A Workbook to Navigate Your Grief -*

ISBN - Paperback: 978-1-0688463-1-1

ISBN - eBook: 978-1-0688463-0-4

Production Manager: Krista Helman
Guided Meditations Narrated and Recorded by: Trina Brunk
Cover Design by: Rebecca Laserna

# Table of Contents

# Introduction



If you've come to this workbook, it's likely that you're either preparing for a loss, navigating one that has already occurred, or supporting someone else through their grief. No matter where you are in this journey, know that you are welcome here, and there is something within these pages to support you.

*To those who have already faced a loss, I offer my deepest sympathy. I can only imagine how difficult this time must be for you.* Grief is a deeply personal experience, and while we all encounter it in different ways, none of us are exempt from this shared part of being human. I encourage you to take your time, reflect gently, and honour your unique path through this process. There is no single answer to healing from grief, and while time may help, it is not the only source of comfort.

As you work through this workbook, you might find it helpful to keep a separate journal to capture any deeper reflections. You can access the guided meditations, by scanning the QR code below. I've also included a few extra journaling pages at the back of this workbook for any thoughts or insights that may need more space or for anything else that arises as we walk this path together.

**Anytime you see a QR code throughout this workbook, scan it to access additional content!**

*For most people, love is the most profound source of pleasure in our lives, while the loss of those whom we love is their most profound source of pain. Hence, love and loss are two sides of the same coin. We cannot have one without risking the other.*

*- Colin Parkes,*
*Love and Loss: The Roots of Grief and Its Complications*

Let's begin with an important truth: this workbook centers on grief and loss, and as you explore these pages, it may stir up feelings related to your own experiences—whether the loss of a human loved one, a pet, or another kind of loss. These emotions might surface unexpectedly, and that's okay. **The key is to be gentle with yourself and prepared for these moments.**

Take a moment now to ground yourself in the space you're in. Feel the support of the chair beneath you, the steadiness of your feet on the floor. Let your eyes wander softly around the room—look to your left, to your right, up at the ceiling, and down at the floor. Take in the boundaries of the room and notice any windows or doors. Remind yourself that right now, you are in a safe space.

Your well-being is so important. **If you find yourself feeling overwhelmed at any point, I encourage you to pause and practice self-care. Step away for a moment, go for a short walk, listen to a calming meditation, or reach out to someone who supports you.**

Now, take a moment to reflect on some of your favourite ways to ground yourself and list them below. Perhaps you'd like to try slow, deep breathing: inhaling gently for 4 seconds, then exhaling for 4, repeating this four times. Or, you might prefer a longer exhale—breathe in for 4 seconds, then let it out slowly for 8. See what feels right for you.

_______________________________________________

_______________________________________________

_______________________________________________

**If you need support while reading this book, list who you can contact. (Visualize that person now)**

_______________________________________________

_______________________________________________

# Growing Pleasant Feelings

Grief often brings with it long periods of discomfort, and while it's important to honour the full depth of your sadness, it's also possible to gently train your mind to notice and nurture moments of joy and gratitude that still exist in daily life.

This activity is here to support you in doing just that, while also helping you build tolerance for all the emotions you may be feeling. Not only can it provide a sense of relief, but it can also help you shift your focus away from overwhelming thoughts or emotions, bringing you back to a place of emotional balance. This way, you can continue moving forward, even in small ways. Just as you might recognize the flutter of butterflies in your stomach as a sign of anxiety, you can also become more aware of what joyful memories and thoughts bring up within you.

By regularly practicing *Growing Pleasant Feelings*, you can increase your body's awareness and build emotional resilience. When you notice yourself feeling overwhelmed, gently return to this practice as a tool to help ground and steady you.

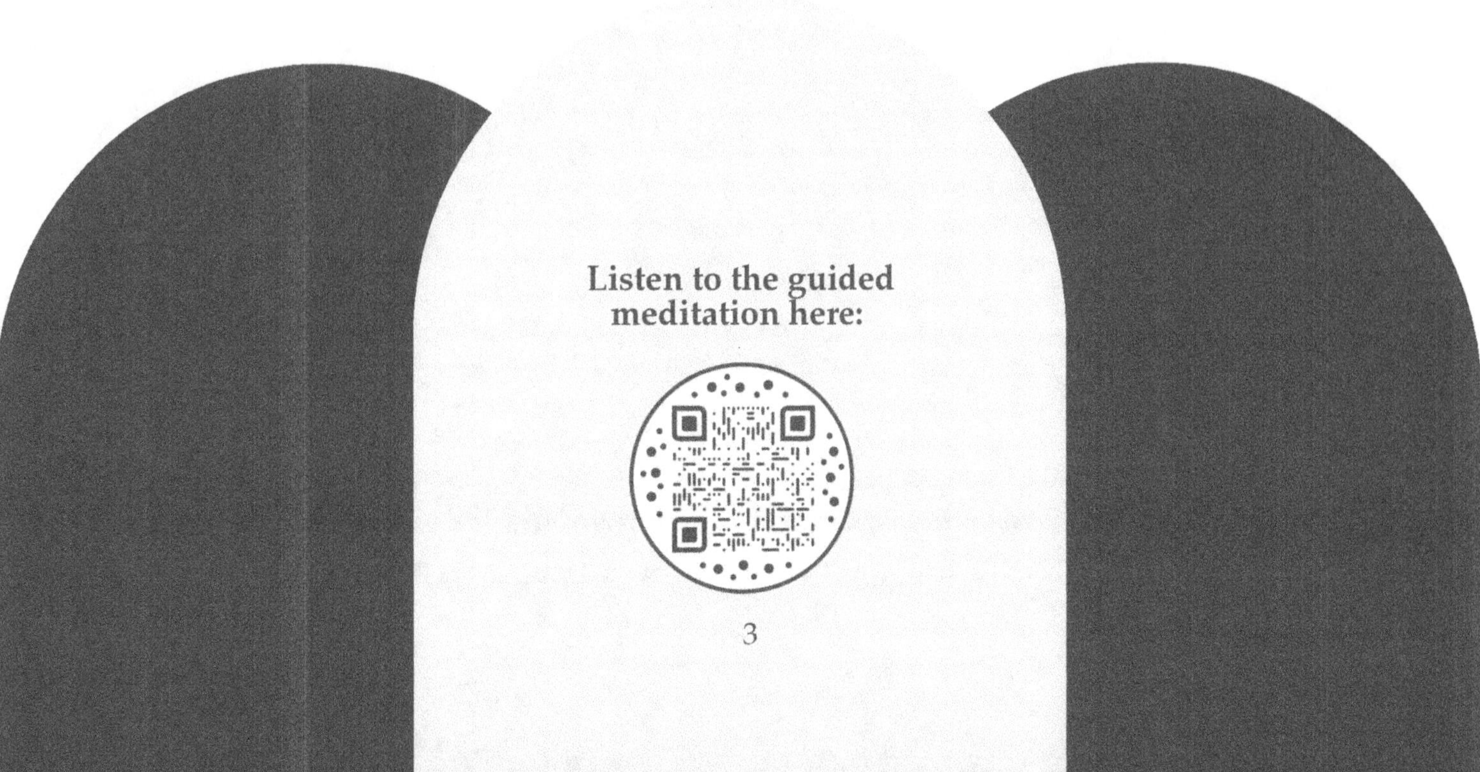

# Self-Care Menu

It's so important to offer yourself a bit of kindness each day. Take a moment now to write down things you can do to care for yourself. These might be simple comforts like curling up in a cozy blanket, sipping your favourite tea, listening to uplifting music, moving your body, resting when you need to, sharing a meal with a friend, or preparing a nourishing meal for yourself. Other ways to care for your mind, body, and soul might include meditation, spending time in nature, or practicing gratitude. Choose whatever feels right for you, and remember that these small moments of care are an essential part of healing.

List 10 ideas of what you can do for self-care:

1

2

3

4

5

6

7

8

9

10

**Keep this list as a menu to refer to when you notice you need it.**
Pick one thing from this list—<u>and do it now!</u>

# Continuing the Bond

When we're in the depths of grief and mourning, our mind can struggle to keep up with the many changes happening in our world. Especially when we've lost someone we love, our mind naturally seeks them—searching for them in space, in time, and in the bond we once shared. It's trying to understand where they've gone, when we might see them again, and how to feel that connection once more.

The comforting news is that, even though our minds may be grappling with this new reality, our connection to our loved one is never truly lost. Even in moments when our pain feels like a barrier, the memories we hold are still alive and vibrant within us. No one, and nothing, can take that away. With time, our mind will begin to accept that our loved one is no longer physically present, and though we may not know if or when we'll be with them again, we can continue to honour and grow that bond.

*To nurture that sense of connection, explore some of the suggestions below:*

## Talking About Them

One way to keep the connection with our loved one vibrant is by actively remembering them. You might choose to talk about them with your support system, sharing stories or memories, or you might prefer a more private reflection through journaling or writing letters to them.

## Photos

Looking at or displaying photos of your loved one can also be a comforting part of this process. These photos are not only a helpful reminder they are no longer physically here, but they also reflect the love and joy they brought into your life. Photos will remind you of the roles your loved one played when they were with you—and the ways the relationship impacted your life in positive ways, even now.

## Take Their View

It's also important to focus on living a fulfilling life, and one way to do this is by imagining what your loved one might say or want you to hear in certain situations. By envisioning their perspective, you can use their wisdom and love as a source of guidance, allowing them to continue being a role model for you as you move forward.

## Talk To Them

You might find comfort in speaking to your loved one, either in your mind or out loud. This simple act can offer a sense of closeness, helping you feel their presence and guidance. In some moments, this may even assist you in working through decisions in your life today, as you imagine what they might say or advise.

## Their Belongings

Holding onto your loved one's belongings can also bring a sense of connection and comfort. However, it's equally okay if you've chosen to part with their things—there's no right or wrong way to navigate this. Your response is deeply personal, and whatever feels best for you is absolutely valid.

## Honouring Them

Rituals, such as funerals or cultural practices like set mourning periods, can offer meaningful ways to honour and remember your loved one. You may also find comfort in visiting places that were special in your relationship, or speaking about them during significant events. Continuing traditions—whether it's hanging a cherished Christmas ornament, setting a place for them at a family dinner, lighting a candle in their memory, or simply pausing to thank them for their legacy—can help you keep their presence vibrant in your heart. There are so many ways to honour their memory, and you can choose what feels most meaningful to you.

## Live with Purpose

You might also find healing in living with purpose, imagining how proud your loved one would be of the choices you've made. Whether you improve your health, embrace a new habit, or visit a place they always wished to go, you are honouring their memory and carrying forward their legacy.

**List some ideas of how you plan to continue the bond.**

_______________________________________________________

_______________________________________________________

_______________________________________________________

_______________________________________________________

Attachment styles exist on a spectrum, and understanding your own can help you better understand your relationship patterns, and improve how you connect with others.

If you tend to have a secure attachment style, it likely stems from an inner sense of security and a worldview that, no matter what happens, life is manageable. This often develops from having a predictable and reliable relationship with a caregiver in childhood.

At the other end of the spectrum, those with a disorganized attachment style may find it more difficult to cope with loss. This pattern can emerge from many experiences, such as feeling stressed or anxious when a caregiver leaves during childhood, especially if it was unclear when or how they would return.

While we are always growing and evolving, the same neural circuits involved in attachment during childhood are often repurposed in our adult relationships as well.

## Read each attachment style description, and then note which one you identify with the most.

### Secure Attachment

If this is your attachment style, you likely feel comfortable with closeness and emotional connection. You can set and respect healthy boundaries without feeling threatened, and you trust that relationships can be reliable. You are not afraid to express your needs or feelings, and you can listen to and respect others' needs. Conflicts can be handled constructively, and you do not fear abandonment.

### Anxious Attachment (Insecure)

If you lean towards this attachment style, you likely seek constant validation and reassurance from others and may worry about your partner leaving you or not loving you. You may look back on relationships and notice you can become overly dependent or clingy, fearing abandonment. The thought of not being in a relationship makes you uncomfortable or anxious. Because of this, your partner's moods and actions are something that you are hyper-attuned to.

### Avoidant Attachment (Insecure)

This attachment style would make you feel uncomfortable with too much closeness or emotional dependency. Independence and self-reliance are things you pride yourself on, and you find it hard to talk about your emotions and needs. Others may have described you as distant or detached in relationships, and you may avoid close or long-term commitment relationships.

**Fearful-Avoidant/Disorganized Attachment (Insecure)**
If you lean toward this attachment style, you likely feel conflicted about relationships. You might feel anxious and avoidant as you desire closeness but fear it. You might be aware that your past negative experiences or unresolved trauma affect your relationships. Trusting others is a struggle, as at your core, you expect betrayal or rejection. This may lead to high emotional ups and downs in your relationships.

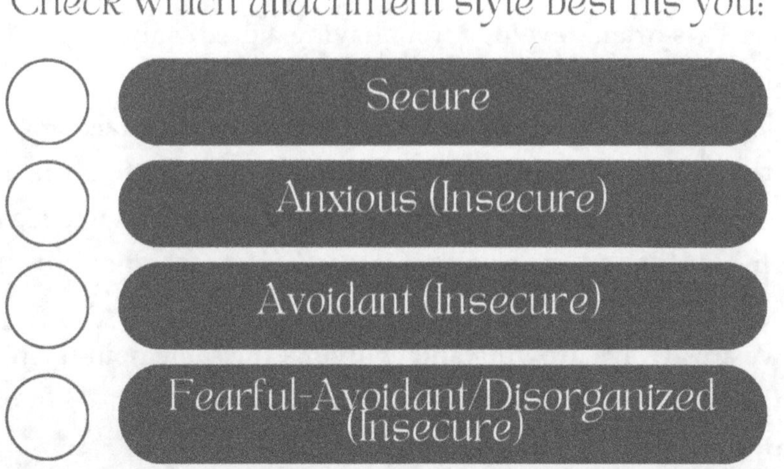


The good news is that you can work towards shifting your relationship patterns—our programming isn't permanent, even as adults!

Here are a few suggestions to help you move toward a more secure attachment style:

- **Start by practising self-awareness and reflection**. Try to identify any patterns in your past relationships and consider how your early life experiences may have shaped them.
- **Working with a therapist can be incredibly helpful** in exploring these patterns and healing trauma. Therapies like Eye Movement Desensitization and Reprocessing (EMDR) can assist with this, while approaches such as the Safe & Sound Protocol (SSP) can improve vagal tone, helping you become more attuned to yourself and others (through neuroception and interoception).
- **Building trusting relationships** is key—this involves following through on commitments, being dependable, and noticing if there is mutual reciprocation in your relationships. If not, reflect on whether the imbalance is on your side or with the other person. Make sure your connections are built on mutual respect and equality.
- **Taking care of yourself is essential for emotional regulation**. Practise self-care by focusing on your physical and mental health—this includes supporting your vagal tone, getting restful sleep, and nourishing yourself with whole foods.

- **Set and respect healthy boundaries** by saying no to requests or situations that don't serve your best interests. Practise expressing your needs, feelings, and boundaries in a safe environment where you feel comfortable.
- **Build emotional intelligence and empathy** by actively trying to see things from another person's perspective. Consciously work on recognizing and understanding your own emotions, and remain open to various viewpoints.
- **Surround yourself with people who have securely attached relationships.** Take time to observe how they interact and consider using their behaviours as a model for your own relationships.
- **Engage in secure connections** by seeking out individuals who display secure attachment behaviours. These relationships may feel different at first, and that's completely normal.
- **Practice patience and self-compassion** as you work on reprogramming your attachment style. Remember that this process takes time and effort, and experiencing setbacks is a natural part of growth. Keep moving toward your goal, and be kind to yourself along the way!

Take a moment to journal and
list ways you can incorporate a shift toward a more
secure attachment pattern into your world.

# Strengthening Vagal Tone

Practising this technique can help you stay present during waves of intense emotions. Just two minutes of deep breathing with a longer exhalation can engage and regulate your vagus nerve, which is the superhighway of information and reactions that supports your survival.

**Vagal tone refers to the activity of the vagus nerve, which plays a key role in regulating your body's stress response. A higher vagal tone is associated with better emotional regulation, resilience, and overall well-being.**

Let's try 10 rounds of breathing using a 4:8 inhalation-to-exhalation ratio. Begin by breathing in through your nose, allowing your belly to expand, and then exhale through your mouth with a gentle blowing sound. The key to this exercise is to breathe deeply and slowly, focusing on the sensation of each breath as it enters your body and then fully leaves it. Regularly practising this can strengthen your vagal tone and help your body and mind process grief more effectively.

**Listen to the guided meditation here:**

# Moving Through the Storm

Being a detective with your feelings is an important step towards clearing the storm clouds of grief. *Explore the following questions that fit with what you are experiencing.*

*Ask yourself if your emotional pain has been so intense that you've had thoughts of hurting yourself or joining your loved one on the other side.*
*If the answer is yes, please contact a bereavement or trauma counsellor.*
*If you are having those thoughts at this moment, please get to an emergency room immediately and tell them you are suicidal—now.*

## Anger

**Anger likely stems from feelings of frustration and a sense of helplessness.** It can be very effective at warding off the sadness. At times, anger can feel intense so this energy needs to go somewhere! You might notice you are releasing it by directing your anger at the deceased, at others, or at yourself. You might be trying to numb your anger, such as using it to work longer hours. If you turn anger inward or resort to unhelpful tactics, you may start feeling depressed, ashamed, or have feelings of guilt.

**How had your anger been showing itself lately?**

**What do you miss about your loved one?**

______________________________________________

______________________________________________

______________________________________________

______________________________________________

______________________________________________

______________________________________________

______________________________________________

______________________________________________

**Regarding their absence, is there something are you angry about? For example, do you feel worse off in life, have more worries, concerns, or problems?**

______________________________________________

______________________________________________

______________________________________________

______________________________________________

______________________________________________

______________________________________________

**Id there anything you don't you miss about your loved one?**

______________________________________________

______________________________________________

______________________________________________

______________________________________________

______________________________________________

______________________________________________

______________________________________________

**Do you feel disappointed about anything in the relationship?**

**What's feeling unfair?**

**What are some ideas to better manage your anger?**

# Guilt

We may experience guilt for various reasons, such as questioning whether we could have provided better medical care, feeling responsible for protecting and caring for a loved one, or believing we should be feeling stronger or different emotions than we are currently experiencing. Often, this guilt is irrational and can hinder our ability to navigate through grief. By understanding our guilt, we can prevent ourselves from becoming stuck in this difficult process. If guilt resonates with you, I encourage you to reflect on the questions below.

**What are you feeling guilt about?**

________________________________________________

________________________________________________

________________________________________________

________________________________________________

________________________________________________

________________________________________________

**What did you do that makes you feel this way?** (*List evidence of your actions*)

________________________________________________

________________________________________________

________________________________________________

________________________________________________

________________________________________________

**Anything else?** (*List all you can think of*)

________________________________________________

________________________________________________

________________________________________________

________________________________________________

________________________________________________

Did you have intent to cause harm?

What was your intention with your actions?

If someone else acted the same as you, what comforting things would you say to them so they could feel less responsible?

What role did others play in this scenario?

It's completely normal to experience fear, anxiety, and helplessness following a death. These feelings may surface as concerns about our ability to thrive independently or as an awakening to the reality of our own mortality. *If you find yourself grappling with these emotions, I invite you to explore the following questions:*

**What do you not have control over that you wish you did?**

**What can you control?**

**How did you manage on your own before the loss?**

**Do you have fears about your own death?**

**What else worries you?**

It makes sense that we may feel lonely after a loved one has died, especially when they lived by our side.

**When do you notice feeling big waves of loneliness?**

_______________________________________________
_______________________________________________
_______________________________________________
_______________________________________________
_______________________________________________

**Who could you reach out to for connection?**
*(Make a list of specific friends/family/animals/professionals/groups)*

_______________________________________________
_______________________________________________
_______________________________________________
_______________________________________________
_______________________________________________

**Is there anything blocking you from reaching out?**

_______________________________________________
_______________________________________________
_______________________________________________
_______________________________________________

**When have you arranged to connect with them?**

_______________________________________________
_______________________________________________
_______________________________________________
_______________________________________________

At the heart of our grief is sadness, and it's important for us to understand the reasons behind our it. *Please take a moment to reflect on the following questions:*

**Who have you lost?**

____________________________________________

____________________________________________

____________________________________________

____________________________________________

**What have you lost?**
*(For example, a companion, a source of purpose, someone to laugh with…)*

____________________________________________

____________________________________________

____________________________________________

____________________________________________

____________________________________________

____________________________________________

**How has or will this change affect the way you live life?** (*Give specific examples*)

____________________________________________

____________________________________________

____________________________________________

____________________________________________

____________________________________________

____________________________________________

____________________________________________

# Colour Breathing

**This activity is a guided meditation designed to foster relaxation and peace.** Meditation can be a valuable tool for navigating grief, as it aids in emotional regulation, reduces stress, and encourages self-reflection.

**Colour Breathing can be adjusted to suit your needs.** You can bring in a colour to help you feel energized or motivated, or perhaps a colour for self-forgiveness. Some people find it helpful to either wear their colour of choice or have this colour in their workspace to help cue them to colour breathe often. **You decide!**

**Listen to the guided meditation here:**

# Drawing Grief

Drawing your grief can help you better
understand your feelings, making it easier to
identify and work through them in a helpful
way. This exercise invites you to identify, feel,
and express your grief.

While you listen to the guided meditation, use the space
below to draw what your grief looks like. Don't worry about
how it looks—just let your emotions guide your creativity!

# Moments of Mastery

It's completely natural for you to feel overwhelmed by grief during times of loss. However, within the depths of your sorrow lie moments of mastery. By exploring your strength and resilience, you can help ground yourself for your journey.

## Strength

Pick a specific memory in your life when you showed remarkable strength. This could be any time of your life, such as when you made a decision to support yourself or others, or simply endured with courage.

**Write down a brief description of this moment of strength.**

________________________________________________

________________________________________________

________________________________________________

________________________________________________

**Identify what made this moment significant.**

________________________________________________

________________________________________________

________________________________________________

________________________________________________

**Give this moment a name.**

________________________________________________

**What emotions did you experience?**

________________________________________________

________________________________________________

**Where do you feel this moment of strength in your body?**

_______________________________________________

_______________________________________________

_______________________________________________

**Notice this feeling in your body as you give yourself a hug. Close your eyes and _slowly_ tap on one arm, then the other, 6 times.**

**Allow yourself to feel your inner strength.**
**Journal how this moment contributed to your ability to cope and carry on.**

_______________________________________________

_______________________________________________

_______________________________________________

_______________________________________________

_______________________________________________

_______________________________________________

_______________________________________________

_______________________________________________

## Empowerment

Recall a moment in your life when you felt a surge of empowerment. This might be when you realized that you had the resilience to continue surviving despite your loss, or that the worst was behind you. Perhaps, this was a moment of clarity and acceptance that marked the beginning of healing, or a celebratory achievement.

**Describe this instance in detail, including the thoughts and sensations you had at the time.**

_______________________________________________

_______________________________________________

_______________________________________________

_______________________________________________

Reflect on what contributed to your sense of empowerment.

Give this moment a title.

How does this moment of empowerment express itself in your body as you think of it now?

Notice this feeling in your body as you give yourself a hug. Close your eyes and *slowly* tap on one arm then the other, 6 times.

Allow yourself to feel this sense of empowerment.
Journal how this moment contributed to your ability to cope and carry on.

*When you need some extra grounding, you can return to these moments at any time!*

# Grief Coping Menu

**Grief affects everyone differently, and there are many ways to cope based on your personal preferences, cultural practices, and beliefs.** *Take a look at the suggestions below, and jot down how and when you might like to try some of these strategies:*

Go for a walk in nature

Exercise

Look through old photos

Listen to uplifting music

Engage in humour or laughter with a movie or a show

Talk to someone

Accept receiving empathy from friends and family

Seek professional support through therapy or join a bereavement support group

Make a date to have lunch with a support person

Create a memorial with photographs or meaningful objects

Wearing clothing that symbolizes mourning or renewal

Journal feelings and thoughts

Cry/experience the full range of emotions

___________________________________________

___________________________________________

___________________________________________

# Confronting Negative Beliefs

When we feel powerless, helpless, or lose a sense of control, our minds can struggle to accept reality. Sometimes, we may cope by blaming or shaming ourselves.

*Take a moment to review the list of negative beliefs below and see if any resonate with you. Then, look at the positive affirmations to help guide you toward self-compassion. Feel free to add your own thoughts and return to this list whenever you need it.*

| Negative Belief | Positive Cognition |
| --- | --- |
| I'm abandoned, alone, invisible. | I can find ways to connect and get my needs met. |
| It's not safe to feel. | I can begin to learn how to manage my feelings. |
| I am unimportant. | I still have value, regardless. |
| I am powerless, helpless, trapped, not in control. | I can learn to accept what I can and cannot control, and the choices in front of me. I can only control what I can, and I can safely let go of some control. |
| I am responsible. | I can learn and accept what my role was/is, and to recognize appropriate responsibility. |
| I should have known better, done something, done more. | I did the best I could with the information and circumstances at the time. |
| I did something wrong; it was my fault. | I did my best. I can learn from my experiences, and to recognize appropriate responsibility. |
| I'm selfish. | I can accept myself for who I am and the decisions I've made. I have value, regardless. |

| Negative Belief Contd. | Positive Cognition Contd. |
| --- | --- |
| I'm vulnerable/can't protect myself. | I can find ways to protect myself. |
| I'm overwhelmed, I can't handle it. | This feeling will not last forever. I can get through it. I have dealt with hard things before. |
| I should feel more than I do. | I'm having a normal human experience. My grief is unique to me, and I can reach out for help if I need it. |
| I shouldn't feel what I do. | It's okay to not feel okay. I'm having a normal human experience. All feelings are welcome, and I can reach out for help if I need it. |
| I must carry on as usual, as though nothing has happened. | I can learn to respect my needs during this human experience. |
| No one understands. | Although my experience is unique to me, there are supportive people/groups/therapists I can reach out to who understand grief. |
|  |  |
|  |  |
|  |  |

# Reflection on Loss & Change

Taking the time to reflect on your loss and the changes it has brought into your life can help you understand its full impact. This awareness is the first step toward rebuilding your connection in your new reality.

Please take as much time as you need to complete this activity. Remember to be gentle with yourself and allow any emotions that arise during this process. If you find it helpful, use deep breathing or other grounding exercises to support you.

*Start by asking yourself, "**What have I lost?**" This includes your relationship with your loved one, your identity, changes in your circumstances, and any other losses you've experienced because of this loss. **Take your time to write down everything that comes to mind.***

Consider what has changed in your life since your loved one died. *Journal any changes or future stressful situations that you're worried about.*

**Write down any past memories of loss that have resurfaced since your recent loss.**

Reflect on your support system. Which friends, family, or other sources of support
are available to you during this time? **Write about the helpful and unhelpful support
you've received, and how it has impacted your grieving process.**
**If you don't have a supportive network, research and write down where you will get
support, such as a grief support group or individual therapy.**

# Container

This Self-Care Moment is a meditation adapted from basic EMDR training. It is being offered to you as a resource for containing big waves of emotion so that you can function day to day during your grief recovery.

You are going to use your imagination to build a container, then temporarily put an unhelpful thought, feeling, or body sensation into it. You cannot put another person or yourself in this container, but you can store how they or your environment makes you feel.

When using this tool, the deal you're making with yourself is that will check in on the thought, feeling, or body sensation at a later time that works for you. When you do this, you will likely notice a reduction in the emotional charge connected to what's in there. If the unhelpful upset does not decrease with intensity, or you are struggling to contain it, it might be time to seek a therapist who specializes in trauma and grief.

## When you have finished building it, draw your container and write down these details on the next page.

What makes your container strong?

How does your secure two-way system work?

How does the comfortable inside of your container make you feel?

What is the name of your container?

## Let's review:

- Container is a tool that temporarily stores thoughts, feelings, or body sensations that are unhelpful in that moment of time.

- It needs to be practiced multiple times a day on smaller things to be able to lift the heavy, upsetting stuff when it comes around.

- Simply notice the body sensation along with any colours, shapes, or words that go with it, and make that lift off your body so it is locked up and comfortable inside.

- Check in on your container at least once a week at a more helpful time to see if the emotional charge is low enough to deal with it.

# Acknowledge, Accept, & Adapt

Take a moment to reflect on the range of emotions you're experiencing. Consider what has changed in your life and what has come about because of these changes. This reflection can help you gain clarity and understand your feelings better.

**What feelings come up when you think of your loved one now?**

**Have you been participating in self-blame or shame?**

**What have you had to adjust to, and how have you accomplished this?**

_______________________________________________
_______________________________________________
_______________________________________________
_______________________________________________
_______________________________________________
_______________________________________________
_______________________________________________
_______________________________________________
_______________________________________________
_______________________________________________
_______________________________________________
_______________________________________________
_______________________________________________
_______________________________________________

**Journal if any feelings seem to be opposite.**
*For example, you may miss them but feel relieved, or love them and feel angry. This is ok!*

_______________________________________________
_______________________________________________
_______________________________________________
_______________________________________________
_______________________________________________
_______________________________________________
_______________________________________________
_______________________________________________
_______________________________________________
_______________________________________________

**What have you resisted and what comes easy with this change?**

Notice if you've been preoccupied with why the death happened, whose fault it was, and who should be responsible moving forward. Perhaps you've been having irrational thoughts such as, "*It should have been me,*" "*I killed them,*" or "*It was my fault.*" Write down what comes up.

**If waiving a magic wand could make you feel different about your circumstances, what would you like life to feel like going forward?**

**What strategies have been helpful for you to cope with your loss so far?**

# Assessing Risk for Complicated Grief

There are several factors that can increase the likelihood of experiencing "complicated grief" after a loss. For each of the factors below, rate yourself on a scale from 0 to 3, based on how much it feels true for you right now. The higher your total score, the higher your risk may be for experiencing complicated grief. *Be gentle and honest with yourself as you go through these questions.*

## 1. Attachment

How close were you to your loved one? How big a role did they play in your life?

0 = Doesn't apply to me
1 = Applies a little
2 = Applies somewhat
3 = Strongly applies to me

## 2. Circumstances of Their Passing

Was their death sudden, violent, or unexpected? Did you witness it? How much did these circumstances affect you?

0 = Doesn't apply to me
1 = Applies a little
2 = Applies somewhat
3 = Strongly applies to me

## 3. Past Experiences

Have you experienced multiple losses or traumas before this one?

0 = Doesn't apply to me
1 = Applies a little
2 = Applies somewhat
3 = Strongly applies to me

## 4. Support System

Do  you feel alone and isolated with your grief? Do you lack of a support system to help you cope with your loss?

- ◯ 0 = Doesn't apply to me
- ◯ 1 = Applies a little
- ◯ 2 = Applies somewhat
- ◯ 3 = Strongly applies to me

## 5. Other Stressors

Are there other major challenges or stressors in your life that are unrelated to your loss?

- ◯ 0 = Doesn't apply to me
- ◯ 1 = Applies a little
- ◯ 2 = Applies somewhat
- ◯ 3 = Strongly applies to me

## 6. Personal Coping Style

Do you tend to bury or avoid your feelings?

- ◯ 0 = Doesn't apply to me
- ◯ 1 = Applies a little
- ◯ 2 = Applies somewhat
- ◯ 3 = Strongly applies to me

## 7. Traumatic Experience

Was your loved one's passing especially traumatic for you? How much did the circumstances of their death impact you?

- ◯ 0 = Doesn't apply to me
- ◯ 1 = Applies a little
- ◯ 2 = Applies somewhat
- ◯ 3 = Strongly applies to me

## 8. Dependency on Daily Living Support

Were you emotionally or physically dependent on your loved one in your daily life? This can also apply if your loss was a pet.

◯ 0 = Doesn't apply to me
◯ 1 = Applies a little
◯ 2 = Applies somewhat
◯ 3 = Strongly applies to me


## 9. Rescue Background

Reflect on if either of you rescued each other. Did your rescue stories influence your bond?

◯ 0 = Doesn't apply to me
◯ 1 = Applies a little
◯ 2 = Applies somewhat
◯ 3 = Strongly applies to me


## 10. Assisted Death Decision

If you had to make decisions about euthanasia or other end-of-life medical choices, how much has this impacted your grief? Do you question the decisions?

◯ 0 = Doesn't apply to me
◯ 1 = Applies a little
◯ 2 = Applies somewhat
◯ 3 = Strongly applies to me


## 11. Unexpected Loss

Was your loss unexpected or sudden?

◯ 0 = Doesn't apply to me
◯ 1 = Applies a little
◯ 2 = Applies somewhat
◯ 3 = Strongly applies to me

## Scoring

**Total your scores for each question to determine your overall risk for complicated grief.**

**0-11: Low Risk**

You may be dealing with typical grief reactions that, although painful, are manageable without professional support. You likely have effective coping mechanisms and support systems in place to help you navigate this difficult time.

**12-22: Moderate Risk**

Certain factors may be complicating your grieving process, making it more challenging to heal. You may benefit from additional support such as grief therapy, or a support group, to help process these emotions and experiences.

**23-33: High Risk**

Your grief may be especially intense or overwhelming, and you could be at higher risk for experiencing complicated grief. You would likely benefit from professional support such as a grief therapist to support you through this challenging time, and help prevent becoming stuck in your grief.

*Remember, this questionnaire is not a diagnostic tool.*
It should only be used to help assess for potential risk factors to provide insight. Consider seeking additional screening.

**Grieving the loss of someone we love is a valid and individual experience. It's okay to accept support. You don't have to go through this alone!**

# What Do You Need to Hear?

Sometimes, even people with the best intentions can say things that end up hurting us during our grieving process. They may think they're being supportive, but their words don't always help. It's important that we are able to feel our emotions without worrying about being told to move past our pain.

This exercise will guide you in identifying how certain comments made you feel and help you explore what you truly needed to hear instead.

*You'll be writing a few different lists, so take your time and reflect on your feelings honestly as you go through this activity.*

**Unhelpful and Hurtful Comments:**
*List three unhelpful or hurtful comments/behaviours someone has done as a result of your loss, even if they were well meaning. For each comment, write how that made you feel.*

Here are some examples of things that might be more helpful for us to hear from our support network. These kinds of statements acknowledge our grief and offer support in a way that helps us feel understood. While no one can take the pain away, hearing these words can make us feel seen and heard without judgment.

*Check off any of the statements below that were said to you, or would have been helpful for you to hear from your support network.*

○ "I'm sorry this is happening."

○ "I'm here for you, no matter what."

○ "It's okay to feel what you're feeling."

○ "I can't imagine how hard this must be for you."

○ "Take all the time you need."

○ "Your grief is valid, and there's no right way to go through this."

○ "Do you want to talk about how you are feeling?"

○ "What were they like? Tell me more."

○ "My favourite memory of them is…"

○ "It's normal to feel whatever you are feeling."

○ "This must be really hard for you."

○ "They were so special to you."

○ "Tell me more about this memory/regret/feeling that's coming up."

○ "My loved one died last year and it was really hard. What is this like for you?"

○ "You're in my thoughts, and I'm thinking of you."

○ "I don't know how you are feeling, but I want you to know I'm here."

○ "I wish I knew what to say right now, but I don't."

○ "I'm coming over to drop off a casserole quickly. There's no need to return the pan."

○ "I thought I'd come over tomorrow, and we'd just go for a walk. Would this be helpful?"

○ "How about I come over on the weekend, and I'll clean your dishes while you rest. You don't need to entertain me."

○ Say nothing. Just sit and listen.

*Write down new ones as well:*

___________________________________________________________

___________________________________________________________

___________________________________________________________

# When is Sadness There?



**When do you notice sadness?**

Think about the times or situations in your life that make you feel sad. This could be when you're alone and thinking about old memories, or when something happens that reminds you of what you've lost.

**Where do you feel it?**

When we are nervous, we often say we have butterflies in our tummy. When we are angry, we might say we have a fire burning in our chest. When experiencing joy we some feel a warmth in their chest. Reflect on how sadness manifests in your body. Does it weigh heavy on your chest, making it difficult to breathe? Do you feel a knot in your stomach or tension in your shoulders? Pay attention the unique sensations with your sadness.

I call this activity *Happiness Files* because it is all about helping our system remember what it's like to focus on accessing positive feelings and sensations. The more we encourage our brain to do this, the easier it gets. This also supports our brain to access the much needed sense of connection to our loved one.



1. **Create a folder that you can easily access on your phone or computer.**

2. **Include photos, video, and audio of happy memories across your lifespan, or that simply spark joy. Some examples include:**
   - **Pleasant images you find online**
   - **Short videos with soothing sounds of nature**
   - **Favourite guided meditations**
   - **Photos of favourite memories**

3. **Come back to this folder often, especially if you are having a sad day. Notice the pleasant shift inside you as your brain invites your neurons to fire and rewire.**

Finding meaning is a key part of your grief journey. When you focus on meaning, it helps your mind let go of what you no longer need to hold onto. This is all about recognizing the love and gratitude your loved one has left behind. As your sadness starts to lift, these joyful connections will often come to mind naturally.

*To help this process, take a moment to write down at least five happy memories you have with your loved one. Think about moments that bring a smile to your face—maybe it's their joyful expression, a fun experience you shared, or the warmth of their hugs.*

This activity shows us that love never goes away, even after death. It is focused on helping you reconnect with your deceased loved one by thinking of a favourite memory of them that sparks joy inside.

Use this tool to honour and celebrate the bond you shared with your loved one, keeping their memory alive in your heart and mind. By actively engaging with the feelings of love, you can start to re-experience a sense of connection, even in their physical absence.

**Practice *Tapping into Love* regularly to nurture your new relationship with them.**

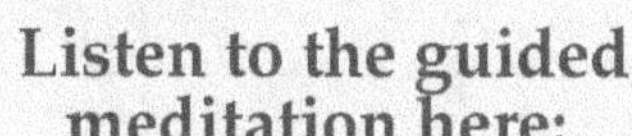

**Listen to the guided
meditation here:**

# Grief Journey Quiz
# Three Phases of Mourning

**The Three Phases of Mourning by Rando (1995) offers a helpful roadmap for navigating the challenges of grief. It outlines how we may experience loss, adjust to a new reality, and find ways to remember and honour our loved one while moving forward. It is normal to slide through each of these phases many time throughout bereavement. This brief quiz is designed to help you understand where you might be in your grief journey.**

*Check off the responses that best reflect how you feel right now. Remember, there are no right or wrong answers; this is just a snapshot of your current experience today.*

## Phase 1 - Avoidance (Past)

I often avoid thinking about my loss, feel overwhelmed.

I struggle to accept the consequences of my loss .

I feel emotionally numb and disconnected when confronted with the impacts of my loss.

## Phase 2 - Confrontation (Present)

Reminders of my loss often lead to intense emotions about how I will deal with the future.

I find it difficult to express thoughts and feelings about my grief because it is painful.

I often find myself longing for the past and wishing things could go back to how they were.

## Phase 3 - Accommodation (Future)

I'm engaging in self-care activities to support my healing.

I'm starting to find new ways to reinvest in my life emotionally, and find satisfaction in daily activities.

I can honour my loved one's memory through actions and find meaning in my relationship with them.

# Scoring:

The more responses you selected for each set of questions determines the likelihood you are in that phase of your grief journey right now.

**Phase 1 - Avoidance (Past)**

**Acknowledging the reality of your loss feels overwhelming most of the time.**

**Phase 2 - Confrontation (Present)**

**Reminders of your loss still trigger intense emotions and pain.**

**Phase 3 - Accommodation (Future)**

**You are finding ways to reinvest in your life emotionally and find meaning in your experiences.**

*Remember that this quiz is a non-scientific tool attempting to capture where you might be right now.*

It is common to move through each phase multiple times. Eventually, we spend most of our time reinvesting in life with meaning and remembering our loved ones while feeling reconnected (Phase 3).

***It's essential to be gentle with yourself and seek support as needed!***

# Navigating the Three Phases of Mourning

Now that you know where you may be in the Three Phases of Mourning by Rando (1995), this activity provides you with strategies to help you cope, depending on where you are today. *Consider if the matching activity instructions are a good fit for you to try.*

## Phase 1: Avoidance

This phase involves feeling overwhelmed by the reality of your loss and struggling to acknowledge it. This phase is important, especially right after a loss.

The goal of these activities are to help you evolve from the unhelpful psychological ties that used to connect you to your loved one, to new ties that are more appropriate for your reality in the present. To do this, you must safely allow yourself to feel your emotions, even if they are painful or uncomfortable.

**Write a list of healthy strategies have helped you cope with overwhelming emotions in the past. It is likely that these can also help you ride the waves of emotions of grief when they come.**

_______________________________________________

_______________________________________________

_______________________________________________

_______________________________________________

**Getting support from friends or family in a safe space is essential. Many of us relied on our loved one for emotional support, so if you do not have someone close to you who can do this, please consider reaching out to a therapist or support group. Write down a plan of who you will trust and rely on for safe emotional support.**

_______________________________________________

_______________________________________________

_______________________________________________

Practice strengthening your vagal tone through meditation, breathing exercises, or other suggestions you find in this book. Write down your favourite grounding exercises and activities.

_______________________________________

_______________________________________

_______________________________________

# Phase 2 - Confrontation

This phase involves confronting the reminders of your loss and leaning to accommodate for the change, which can bring intense emotions. The goal of these activities is for you to express your thoughts and feelings about your loss, and practice differentiating past experiences from the present. It's key to practice self-compassion and remind yourself that it's okay to feel whatever emotions arise. If you notice a wave of emotions you can repeat in your mind, "It is acceptable and manageable for me to feel. My pain has a purpose, and I am resilient."

**Journal how you have been coping with the pain of your grief. Are there any activities or practices that have helped you express yourself? Are there any that are numbing or blocking your grieving process? What are some things you'd like to try the next time you have a big wave of grief?**

**Think about the legacy of your loved one. Find a photo or bring to mind a positive memory of your loved one, and thank them out loud for the life lessons and gifts they gave you in their relationship with you.**

**Practice using your vagal tone toolbox, reaching out for support, and self-care.**

# Phase 3 - Accommodation

This phase involves living adaptively to your new reality without fear of forgetting your past, and finding satisfaction in life again. The goal of these activities is to help you reinvest in your life emotionally, and find new meaning in your connection.

**We cannot go through grief alone! It can be healing to connect with others who are experiencing similar losses. Do a quick online search to see what pet bereavement support groups or online communities exist.**

**Write how you envision reinvesting in your new life. How would you like to be living your life moving forward? How would your loved one have wanted to you be living it?**

_______________________________________________

_______________________________________________

_______________________________________________

_______________________________________________

_______________________________________________

_______________________________________________

**How can you honour the life of your loved one? Perhaps it is visiting a place you visited often together, or place you both wanted to visit. Maybe it is hanging a special Christmas ornament on the tree, or putting up a photo of them in the main living space, or hanging their dog tag in their favourite dog park. Creating memory boxes or scrapbooks are also great ways to honour our loved one. Add this plan to our calendar.**

**Having a menu is always helpful! List self-care practices can you incorporate into your daily routine to support your healing journey.**

_______________________________________________

_______________________________________________

_______________________________________________

_______________________________________________

_______________________________________________

_______________________________________________

*These are just a few suggestions, and as long as we are participating in
bereavement without harm to ourselves or others, there is no wrong way to grieve.
We need to take things one day at a time, be gentle with ourselves.*

The questionnaire for this exercise is designed to help you assess whether you might be in complicated grief, meaning, stuck in the Three Phases of Mourning.

This questionnaire has been provided by *The Hospice Support Fund*. It is not diagnostic, but it helps give an idea of whether it's time to reach out for professional support.

*Please Note: We've recreated this questionnaire to make it user-friendly and possible for you to complete within the workbook.*
*If you would like to access the original version which includes detailed information on diagnosis', treatment options and the references, you can do so at the link below.*

# Inventory for Complicated Grief

For each item, describe how you feel right now using one of these five terms:
• Never • Rarely • Sometimes • Often • Always

| | |
|---|---|
| 1. I think about this person so much that it's hard for me to do the things I normally do... | |
| 2. Memories of the person who died upset me.... | |
| 3. I feel I cannot accept the death of the person who died... | |
| 4. I feel myself longing for the person who died... | |
| 5. I feel drawn to places and things associated with the person who died... | |
| 6. I can't help feeling angry about his/her death... | |

| 7. I feel disbelief over what happened... | |
| 8. I feel stunned or dazed over what happened... | |
| 9. Ever since s/he died, it is hard for me to trust people... | |
| 10. Ever since s/he died, I feel like I have lost the ability to care about other  people or I feel distant from people I care about... | |
| 11. I have pain in the same area of my body or have some of the same symptoms  as the person who died... | |
| 12. I go out of my way to avoid reminders of the person who died... | |
| 13. I feel that life is empty without the person who died... | |
| 14. I hear the voice of the person who died speak to me... | |
| 15. I see the person who died stand before me... | |
| 16. I feel that it is unfair that I should live when this person died... | |
| 17. I feel bitter over this person's death... | |
| 18. I feel envious of others who have not lost someone close... | |
| 19. I feel lonely a great deal of the time ever since s/he died... | |

## Continue to next page to score this questionnaire..

# Scoring

**Add up the number of answers you provided for each term below.**

| | # of Times Answered | | Score Per Term |
|---|---|---|---|
| Number of "NEVER" answers | | X 0 | |
| Number of "RARELY" answers | | X 1 | |
| Number of "SOMETIMES" answers | | X 2 | |
| Number of "OFTEN" answers | | X 3 | |
| Number of "ALWAYS" answers | | X 4 | |

TOTAL SCORE

**25 or less** unlikely CG

**26-30** probable CG

**31 or higher** likely CG

*Remember, this questionnaire is not a diagnostic tool.*
*To learn more about this questionnaire*
*and to visit the original source, please visit:*

https://static1.squarespace.com/static/5fe278aec01e323d6cc0bc73/t/60f98fccaa32ea2fffbf31b5/1626968012585/complicated-grief-report.pdf.

Making a memory book is something that can be done as a family or alone. This symbol of love can be left out to be seen as a reminder of the shared connection, and as a tool to reminisce, mourn, and adapt to the new world. *Suggestions to include:*

- **Drawings of memories**

- **Written stories of fun moments**

- **Photos of their life**

- **Poems from the heart**

- **Letters to them**

## Write down your ideas below.

# Letting Go of "What-Ifs"

This activity is designed to help you process and release the burden of "what-if" thinking and guilt, allowing you to focus on honouring the memory of your loved one with love and compassion.

1. **Find a quiet and comfortable space, then take deep breaths to centre yourself.**
2. **Follow the examples in the table to complete the "what-if" scenarios related to your feelings of guilt, shame, and anger.**
3. **Add as many what-ifs as you wish. Acknowledge these thoughts without judgment and write compassionate and realistic responses.**
4. **Visualize releasing these "what-if" thoughts like balloons, letting them drift away.**
5. **Take a breath in, then all the way out, and give yourself a hug as you let go.**

| Unhelpful Thought | Helpful Thought |
| --- | --- |
| What if I had come home earlier? | I did the best I could with the information I had. |
| What if I had taken them to the vet sooner? | I can begin to learn how to manage my feelings. |
| What if I had spent more money on their care? | I provided the best care I could afford and prioritized their comfort and health best I could. |
|  |  |
|  |  |
|  |  |

# Sunlight Boost

A simple way to improve sleep and well-being is by getting sunlight early in the morning, even if it's not right at sunrise. This activity can have significant benefits for our overall health by aligning our body's hormones and neurotransmitters.

- Unless you have a medical reason to stay out of light, **try spending 10 to 30 minutes under a full-spectrum bright light or in sunlight.** This can help regulate your body's internal clock and hormone levels like cortisol and melatonin. It's okay to wear eyeglasses or contacts with UV protection – they won't hinder the benefits.

- **When you wake up in the morning, make sure your room is well-lit with bright lights if the sun isn't up yet.** Once the sun rises or there's natural light, position yourself near a window or step outside to get direct sunlight exposure. Avoid looking directly at the sun or any excessively bright light!

- **Use this time for activities like reading, stretching, or simply enjoying the outdoors.** The idea is for your skin and eyes to absorb the light, so stay away from your phone at this time.

- **Make this a practice for 10 to 30 minutes daily** to potentially help regulate hormone and neurotransmitter levels, boost daytime alertness, and improve your nighttime sleep quality.

- **Journal your energy levels, mood, and sleep patterns** to notice the impact of morning light exposure on your well-being.

# Gratitude Rock

*Gratitude Rock* is based on the idea that what you focus on can grow new connections in your brain. Many of my clients have found that this exercise significantly boosts their ability to be present and helps them discover purpose and value in their lives. It's a great way to increase your tolerance for feelings and cultivate positivity. By intentionally focusing on the things you're grateful for, you can train your brain to notice more of the good things in your life. It also helps you to rewire your brain to be in the present moment.

Think of it like children sliding down a toboggan hill. With each ride, they go faster down the same slippery part of the hill. Our brains work similarly: the more we encourage certain thoughts or behaviours, the more natural they become. Practicing gratitude is like asking yourself to slide down the sunny side of the toboggan hill, even if it feels a bit difficult at first! The initial attempts might be frustrating, but the more you practice, the easier it gets.

Try to incorporate this technique into your daily routine for at least a week, and you may notice a positive shift in how you feel about your world. As an alternative to using a rock, you can also use a coloured hair elastic around your phone. If the colour of the elastic matches what you visualized during the Colour Breathing meditation, even better!

*Gratitude Rock can transform your outlook on life*
*and enhance your overall sense of connection in the present.*

# Letter of Love

Sometimes, it can be hard to express what we're feeling or to imagine where our loved one is now. Writing a structured letter can be a meaningful way to reflect on your emotions, honour their memory, and say goodbye.

Feel free to use the template below to guide your writing. Take your time with each section and let your thoughts flow. Remember, this letter is for you, so write whatever feels right.

Dear ___________________,

I want to tell you what it was like for me when you started your next journey…

Thinking about you brings up feelings of...

When I lost you, I lost…

I miss you the most when …

_______________________________________________

_______________________________________________

_______________________________________________

_______________________________________________

You made my life better when…

_______________________________________________

_______________________________________________

_______________________________________________

_______________________________________________

What I miss the most about you is….

_______________________________________________

_______________________________________________

_______________________________________________

_______________________________________________

If only I could have told you...

_______________________________________________

_______________________________________________

_______________________________________________

_______________________________________________

It's difficult for me to accept that we didn't get to...

_______________________________________________

_______________________________________________

_______________________________________________

I wish…

My favourite times with you were when…

Even though you're no longer here, I will always carry your memory with me, especially when...

I'm slowly coming to terms with your absence by...

I find comfort in knowing that...

I want you to know that…

___________________________________________________

___________________________________________________

___________________________________________________

___________________________________________________

___________________________________________________

Thank you for being such an important part of my life and teaching me...

___________________________________________________

___________________________________________________

___________________________________________________

___________________________________________________

___________________________________________________

I continue to carry your memory with me, reminding me to…

___________________________________________________

___________________________________________________

___________________________________________________

___________________________________________________

___________________________________________________

I hope your next journey brings you love and light. I imagine you now as…

___________________________________________________

___________________________________________________

___________________________________________________

___________________________________________________

___________________________________________________

You will forever hold a special place in my heart because...

___________________________________________________

___________________________________________________

___________________________________________________

# Practicing Being Present

As you navigate through your grief, it's important to be present and connected to your emotions and surroundings. You can acknowledge and embrace your feelings of loss without getting lost in memories or wishing for a different reality.

*Let's ground in the present moment to prepare for staying grounded when big waves of emotion come. You can write about your experiences afterward to reflect.*

**Listen to the guided meditation here:**

# Hello Again

Visualizing talking to our loved one can be a very powerful technique. In this activity, you will have an opportunity to imagine having an interaction with them in the present. The key here is to speak to them, not about them.

Although tempting, please skip this exercise for now if  you are early in your grieving process where you are feeling unsafe with yourself, numb, needing additional support for your grief or your mental health. Asking your therapist to guide you through this exercise may be an option.

*Listen to the guided meditation and use the space below:*

**What do you want them to understand about their death and your relationship?**

________________________________________________

________________________________________________

________________________________________________

________________________________________________

________________________________________________

________________________________________________

________________________________________________

**What did your relationship mean to you?**

________________________________________________

________________________________________________

________________________________________________

________________________________________________

________________________________________________

**What do you want to say about any regrets you might have regarding the relationship?**

**What do you wish you could have said to them while they were alive?**

# After Death Communication Reflection Worksheet



These are examples of scientifically documented *After-Death Communication (ADC)*. Across our lifespan, humans have been experiencing ADC. Stories of them can be found across cultures, beliefs, and states of health. The research shows that experiencers tend to find closure and connection through them, so exploring the details is important.

**If you've experienced an ADC, this activity helps you to look deeper into it.** Your experience is unique and valid, and it's essential to honour your feelings and reactions. Take time to reflect on your ADC, and practice self-care as needed. In addition to your support network, a therapist can be helpful with making meaning of experiences.

*Journal your experience on the next few pages to document your journey.*

## Type of ADC

**Visual ADC:** Describe any visual sightings or images you had.

**Auditory ADC:** Detail any sounds or voices you heard, this might involve hearing their voice or specific sounds you associate with them.

**Tactile ADC:** Explain any physical sensations or feelings of touch associated with your experience, such as a sense of warmth, pressure, or the feeling of a hug.

**Olfactory ADC:** Specify any scents or smells that reminded you of the deceased at the time. This might include their perfume or a favourite cooking smell.

**Sentient ADC:** Describe any sense of presence or intuitive feelings of connection you had with the deceased. This could involve feeling their energy or presence.

# Description of the ADC

**Describe additional details of what happened during your ADC and how it unfolded. Include any sensations, emotions, thoughts, or messages you experienced. Be as detailed as possible. For example, describe where you were, what you were doing, and how the ADC unfolded.**

**Comforted:** Explain how the experience brought you comfort or reassurance. Describe any feelings of warmth or peace that accompanied your ADC.

**Supported:** Describe any feelings of support or guidance you received from your ADC. This might include a sense of encouragement or understanding.

**Relieved:** Detail any sense of relief or ease you felt during your ADC.

**Scared:** If you experienced fear or discomfort, specify the nature of your apprehension. Describe any factors that contributed to your feelings of fear.

**Intruded Upon:** If the ADC felt intrusive or unsettling, describe how it impacted you. Explain any feelings of unease or disruption caused by the experience.

**Other:** Fill in if your feelings don't match the options above.

**Fostered a sense of connection:** Describe any feelings of closeness or connection you experienced, such as a sense of continuity or understanding.

**Deeper understanding:** Describe what the messages or symbols you received meant for you?

**Assisted the grieving process:** Detail how your ADC has contributed to your healing or acceptance of your loss.

**Changes in perspective:** Such as a renewed sense of emotional resilience. Consider how it may have influenced your beliefs or outlook on life and death.

**Shared the experience with others:** Detail any conversations or interactions you had about your ADC. Describe any reactions or responses you received from others.

**Reflected on the meaning:** Explain any additional insights or realizations you gained from your experience.

**Experienced fear or discomfort:** If your ADC triggered fear or discomfort, explain how you coped with it. Describe any strategies or coping mechanisms you used, or can use, to manage your ongoing emotions.

**I need to talk to someone about the experience:** Specify if you think you require professional support or counselling. Consider reaching out to a therapist or grief support group for guidance.

**I'm seeking validation or understanding:** Detail any need for validation or reassurance regarding your experience. Consider reaching out to friends, family, or support groups who can offer empathy and understanding.

**I'm still exploring the meaning of my ADC:** Summarize what your experience meant for you or discuss your experience with a trusted confidant.

**I'm coping with fear or discomfort:** Explain any specific coping strategies or support you have available to you to manage your emotions. List self-care techniques and who you plan to reach out to for support.

**Other:** Specify anything you think you may need, such as resources, spiritual guidance, or further exploration of the afterlife on your own.

# Reflection & Moving Forward

Take a moment to reflect on the range of emotions you've experienced, what has shifted, and how those changes have impacted you. You've already done a lot of work in this workbook, so let's check in with yourself and see if anything has changed.

*Take some time to notice any differences in how you feel now compared to when you started. What emotions have come up for you? What has changed, and how have those changes affected you? This is a good time to pause, reflect, and acknowledge your progress.*

# Circle of Love

This guided meditation offers a gentle space for you to connect with the warmth of loving energy. Both giving and receiving love can bring comfort, especially during times of grief. As you visualize loving beings or entities forming a circle around you, it serves as a reminder that you are supported and connected, even if those people or beings aren't physically present

*Take your time with this meditation,*
*and let yourself fully experience the circle of love and support surrounding you.*

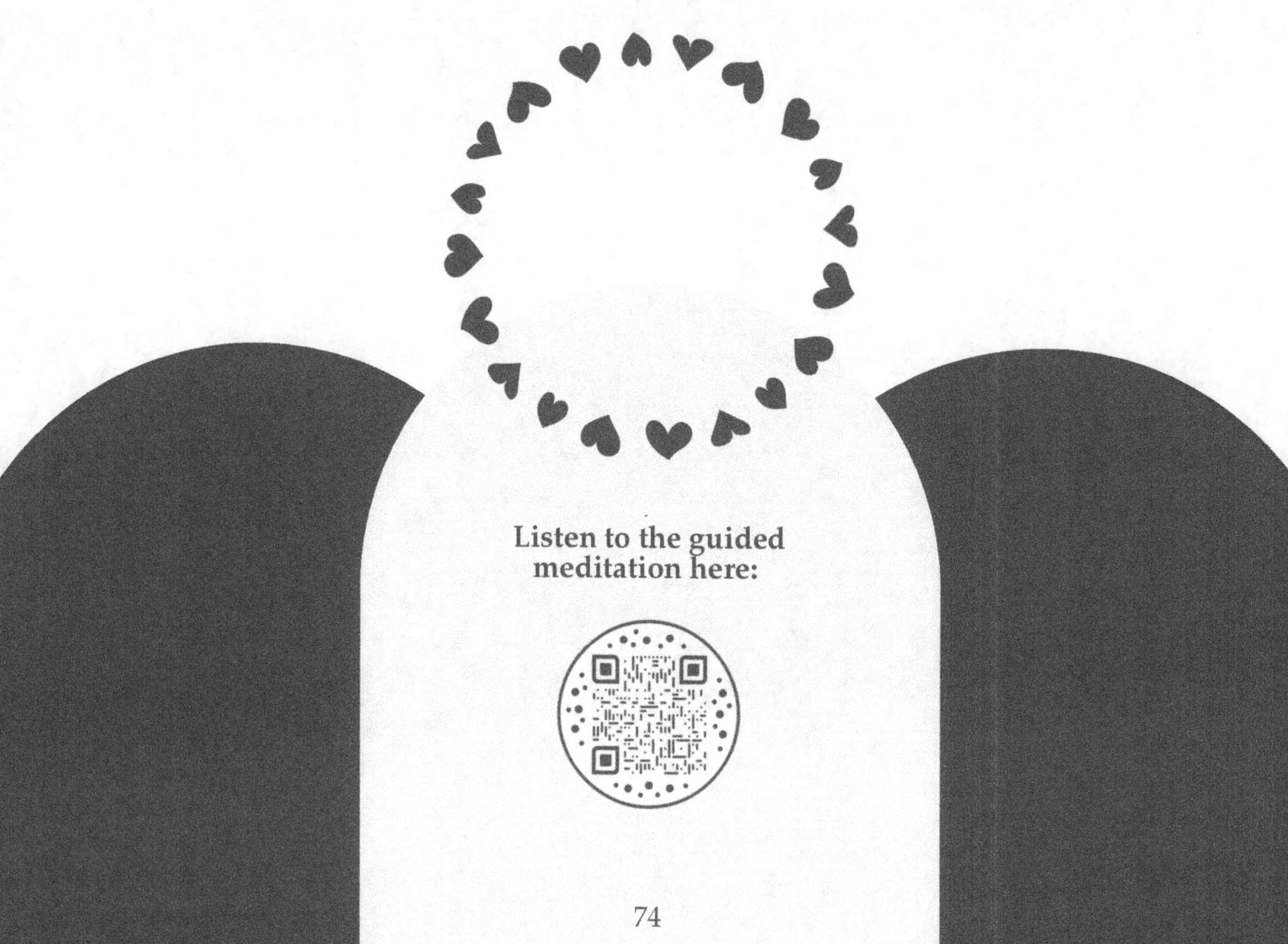

# About the Author

**Krista Helman** is a compassionate therapist, author, and social worker based in Canada. With years of clinical experience, she is the founder and Director of the Trauma & Grief Institute (TGI), where she leads a team offering therapy, training, and community-based healing grounded in evidence-based and holistic practices.

She is the developer of the EMDR-GRIEF protocol, an integrative approach to processing grief using EMDR therapy, and she provides training for clinicians internationally. A sought-after speaker and presenter, Krista offers professional workshops, online courses, and transformative retreats for both the public and mental health professionals.

Krista is the author of Over the Rainbow: The Love, Loss, and Legacy of Your Dog, a heartfelt guide blending therapeutic strategies, psychoeducation, and personal stories for those mourning the loss of a beloved pet. She has also published Self-Care Moments: A Workbook to Navigate Your Grief.

While her expertise spans a wide range of therapeutic areas, Krista is particularly passionate about grief, trauma, and the human search for meaning. She has a deep interest in the phenomenon of after-death communication (ADC) and is committed to destigmatizing scientifically supported experiences that are often misunderstood.

When not working, Krista enjoys spending time with her family—both human and furry—and finds peace in the healing rhythms of nature.

# Krista Helman's
# Keynotes & Workshops

Krista would be pleased to receive your invitation to speak or present at your event. Her engaging presentations and interactive workshops offer accessible insights and practical strategies rooted in the latest mental health practices.

As the Director of the Trauma & Grief Institute (TGI) and the developer of the EMDR-GRIEF protocol, Krista leads a variety of workshops, classes, and training opportunities for both the public and clinicians. These offerings span a wide range of topics, from trauma and grief-specific content to general wellness, emotional resilience, and mind-body integration.

Krista presents at professional conferences and is particularly passionate about engaging with diverse audiences, including healthcare and veterinary professionals, workplace teams seeking a healthier culture, caregivers and frontline workers facing burnout, and organizations seeking impactful education on grief, trauma, and wellness.

She also holds a special interest in the phenomenon of after-death communication (ADC) and is committed to destigmatizing scientifically supported human experiences that remain poorly understood. Her offerings continue to evolve alongside her leadership at TGI, with a focus on compassion, connection, and evidence-based care.

**Krista is particularly interested in engaging with audiences such as:**

- Professionals looking for additional training.
- Event organizers focusing on trauma, grief, or wellness.
- Employers seeking a more positive workplace culture.
- Professionals and caregivers battling burnout.
- Frontline workers exposed to adversity.
- Veterinary professionals wanting to learn how to support their patients and owners regarding grief and loss.

# See what others have to say!

*"Krista is a phenomenal presenter. She speaks from a perspective of someone who understands intimately her topics and not just from a theoretical perspective. She makes topics easy to understand and then apply in practice. She is knowledgeable, approachable and an enjoyable presenter to listen to."*

**- Julie Marquis, RP**

*"Krista is engaging and impactful. Even as a seasoned therapist I learned a lot from her well-researched presentation."*

**- Alison Sharp, RSW, LCSW**

*"Krista's presentations are well-researched and organized. She is clear, personable, and engaging. She integrates theory into practice with plenty of examples, videos, and opportunities for learners to practice the skills discussed. I have learned a lot from Krista and value her knowledge regarding EMDR, parts work, and grief counselling."*

**- Emily Davison, MSW, RSW**

**For more information, please visit: <u>kristahelman.com</u>**

# References


Beder, Joan. "Loss of the Assumptive World—How We Deal with Death and Loss." *OMEGA - Journal of Death and Dying* 50, no. 4 (June 2005): 255–65. https://doi.org/10.2190/gxh6-8vy6-bq0r-gc04.

Beischel, J. Spontaneous, Facilitated, Assisted, and Requested After-Death Communication Experiences and their Impact on Grief. Accessed April 6, 2024. https://www.researchgate.net/publication/334330476_Spontaneous_Facilitated_Assisted_and_Request ed_After-Death_Communication_Experiences_and_their_Impact_on_Grief_Peer- reviewed_referenced_commentary.

Bohlmeijer, Ernst T., Jannis T. Kraiss, Philip Watkins, and Marijke Schotanus-Dijkstra. "Promoting Gratitude as a Resource for Sustainable Mental Health: Results of a 3-Armed Randomized Controlled Trial up to 6 Months Follow-Up." *Journal of Happiness Studies* 22, no. 3 (May 7, 2020): 1011–32. https://doi.org/10.1007/s10902-020-00261-5.

Botkin, Allan L., and R. Craig Hogan. *Induced after-death communication: A miraculous therapy for grief and loss*. Charlottesville, VA: Hampton Roads, 2014.

Bretherton, Inge. "The Origins of Attachment Theory: John Bowlby and Mary Ainsworth." *A century of developmental psychology.*, 1994, 431–71. https://doi.org/10.1037/10155-029.

Claire Place Veterinary Hospice. "Do Pets Grieve?" Claire Place Veterinary Hospice Mobile Services, January 4, 2019. https://www.hospicevet.com/do-pets-grieve/.

Cotter, Prudence, Larissa Meysner, and Christopher William Lee. "Participant Experiences of Eye Movement Desensitization and Reprocessing vs. Cognitive Behavioural Therapy for Grief: Similarities and Differences." *European Journal of Psychotraumatology* 8, no. sup6 (October 9, 2017). https://doi.org/10.1080/20008198.2017.1375838.

Dent-Smyth, Kelly. "The Acute Stress Syndrome Stabilization Remote Individual (ASSYST-Ri) for Telemental Health Counseling after Adverse Experiences." Psychology and Behavioral Science International Journal 16, no. 2 (January 20, 2021). https://doi.org/10.19080/pbsij.2021.16.555932.

Elsaesser et al. "Investigation of the Phenomenology and Impact of Spontaneous and Direct After-Death
Communications (ADCs): Research Findings." adcrp. Accessed April 6, 2024.
https://www.adcrp.org/project.

Field, Nigel P., and Charles Filanosky. "Continuing Bonds, Risk Factors for Complicated Grief, and Adjustment to
Bereavement." *Death Studies* 34, no. 1 (December 16, 2009): 1–29.
https://doi.org/10.1080/07481180903372269.

Girianto, Pria Wahyu, Dhina Widayati, and Syahdila Sabrina Agusti. "Butterfly Hug to Reduce Anxiety on Elderly."
*Jurnal Ners dan Kebidanan (Journal of Ners and Midwifery)* 8, no. 3 (December 26, 2021): 295–300.
https://doi.org/10.26699/jnk.v8i3.art.p295-300.

Hall, Christopher. "Bereavement Theory: Recent Developments in Our Understanding of Grief and Bereavement."
*Bereavement Care* 33, no. 1 (January 2, 2014): 7–12. https://doi.org/10.1080/02682621.2014.902610.

Helman, Krista. *Over the Rainbow: The Love, Loss, & Legacy of Your Dog.* Ottawa, ON: FernAura, 2024.

Hewson, Helen, Niall Galbraith, Claire Jones, and Gemma Heath. "The Impact of Continuing Bonds Following
Bereavement: A Systemic Review." *Death Studies*, June 19, 2023, 1–14.
https://doi.org/10.1080/07481187.2023.2223593.

Hoggan, Sarah. "Pet Loss Grief; the Pain Explained | Sarah Hoggan DVM | TEDxTemecula." YouTube, November
10, 2022. https://www.youtube.com/watch?v=TkJGhQANjZo&list=PLu8TmV21M5S-
gaO8eIy6ytwHSajAcfDH7&index=3.

Hoggan, Sarah. "The Emotional Costs of Euthanasia | Sarah Hoggan DVM | TEDxTemecula." YouTube, October
25, 2019. https://www.youtube.com/watch?v=Jh-KKjIJHfk&list=PLu8TmV21M5S-
gaO8eIy6ytwHSajAcfDH7&index=4.

Hornsveld, Hellen K., Frieda Landwehr, Willeke Stein, Margaretha P. Stomp, Monique A. Smeets, and Marcel A.
van den Hout. "Emotionality of Loss-Related Memories Is Reduced After Recall Plus Eye Movements
but Not After Recall Plus Music or Recall Only." *Journal of EMDR Practice and Research* 4, no. 3
(August 2010): 106–12. https://doi.org/10.1891/1933-3196.4.3.106.

The Hospice Support Fund. Complicated Grief. Accessed April 7, 2024.
https://static1.squarespace.com/static/5fe278aec01e323d6cc0bc73/t/60f98fccaa32ea2fffbf31b5/162696
8012585/complicated-grief-report.pdf.

Huberman, Andrew. "The Science & Process of Healing from Grief | Huberman Lab Podcast #74." YouTube, May
    30, 2022. https://www.youtube.com/watch?v=dzOvi0Aa2EA.


James, John, and Russell Friedman. *The grief recovery handbook: The action program for moving beyond death,
    divorce, and other losses including health, career, and faith.* New York, NY: William Morrow, an
    imprint of HarperCollins Publishers, 2017.

Jarero, Ignacio, Lucina Artigas, and Marilyn Luber. "The EMDR Protocol for Recent Critical Incidents: Applications
    in a Disaster Mental Health Continuum of Care Context." *Journal of EMDR Practice and Research* 5,
    no. 3 (2011): 82–94. https://doi.org/10.1891/1933-3196.5.3.82.

Jarero, Ignacio. "Randomized Controlled Clinical Trial on the Provision of the EMDR-PRECI to Family Caregivers
    of Patients with Autism Spectrum Disorder." *Psychology and Behavioral Science International Journal*
    11, no. 1 (March 19, 2019). https://doi.org/10.19080/pbsij.2019.11.555802.

Jarero, Ignatio. AIP Model-Based Acute Trauma and Ongoing Traumatic Stress Theoretical Conceptualization,
    2022. https://www.researchgate.net/publication/322144707_AIP_model-
    based_Acute_Trauma_and_Ongoing_Traumatic_Stress_Theoretical_Conceptualization.


Jordan, John. "Guided Imaginal Conversations with the Deceased." Techniques of Grief Therapy, May 23, 2012,
    282–85. https://doi.org/10.4324/9780203152683-86.
Kessler, David. Finding meaning: The sixth stage of grief. New York, NY: Scribner, 2020.


"Kidsgrief.Ca." Kids Grief. Accessed June 11, 2024. https://kidsgrief.ca/.


Kubler-Ross, Elisabeth. *On death and dying: What the dying have to teach doctors, nurses, clergy and their own
    families.* Scribner, 2014.
Luber, Marilyn. "Protocol for Excessive Grief." *Journal of EMDR Practice and Research* 6, no. 3 (2012): 129–35.
    https://doi.org/10.1891/1933-3196.6.3.129.


McCormick, B, and N Tassell-Matamua. "After-Death Communication: A Typology of Therapeutic Benefits."
    *Journal of Near-Death Studies* 34, no. 3 (2016). https://doi.org/10.17514/jnds-2016-34-3-p151-172.

McDonnell, F. EMDR and Bereavement, 2009. http://www.emdryorkshire.org/resource/FokkinaMcDonnell-
    Workshop5.pdf.

McInerny, Norma. "We Don't 'Move on' from Grief. We Move Forward with It | Nora McInerny | Ted." YouTube,
    April 25, 2019. https://www.youtube.com/watch?v=khkJkR-ipfw&list=PLu8TmV21M5S-
    gaO8eIy6ytwHSajAcfDH7&index=2.

Mead, Nathaniel. "Benefits of Sunlight: A Bright Spot for Human Health." *Environmental Health Perspectives* 116, no. 4 (April 2008). https://doi.org/10.1289/ehp.116-a160.

Menon, Sukanya B., and C. Jayan. "Eye Movement Desensitization and Reprocessing: A Conceptual Framework." *Indian Journal of Psychological Medicine* 32, no. 2 (July 2010): 136–40. https://doi.org/10.4103/0253-7176.78512.

Meysner, Larissa, Prudence Cotter, and Christopher W. Lee. "Evaluating the Efficacy of EMDR with Grieving Individuals: A Randomized Control Trial." *Journal of EMDR Practice and Research* 10, no. 1 (2016): 2–12. https://doi.org/10.1891/1933-3196.10.1.2.

Mol, Saskia S., Arnoud Arntz, Job F. Metsemakers, Geert-Jan Dinant, Pauline A. Vilters-van Montfort, and J. André Knottnerus. "Symptoms of Post-Traumatic Stress Disorder after Non-Traumatic Events: Evidence from an Open Population Study." *British Journal of Psychiatry* 186, no. 6 (June 2005): 494–99. https://doi.org/10.1192/bjp.186.6.494.

Neimeyer, Robert. *New techniques of grief therapy: Bereavement and beyond*. New York: Routledge, 2022.

Nuwer, Rachel. "The 'rainbow Bridge' Has Comforted Millions of Pet Parents. Who Wrote It?" Animals, February 22, 2023. https://www.nationalgeographic.com/animals/article/rainbow-bridge-poem-pet-death-mourning-origin-revealed.

O'Connor, Mary-Frances, David Wellisch, Annette Stanton, Naomi Eisenberger, Michael Irwin, and Matthew Lieberman. "Craving Love? Enduring Grief Activates Brain's Reward Center." *NeuroImage* 42, no. 2 (August 2008): 969–72. https://doi.org/10.1016/j.neuroimage.2008.04.256.

O'Connor, Mary-Frances, David Wellisch, Annette Stanton, Richard Olmstead, and Michael Irwin. "Diurnal Cortisol in Complicated and Non-Complicated Grief: Slope Differences across the Day." *Psychoneuroendocrinology* 37, no. 5 (May 2012): 725–28. https://doi.org/10.1016/j.psyneuen.2011.08.009.

O'Connor, Mary-Frances, John Allen, and Alfred Kaszniak. "Emotional Disclosure for Whom?" *Biological Psychology* 68, no. 2 (February 2005): 135–46. https://doi.org/10.1016/j.biopsycho.2004.04.003.

O'Connor, Mary-Frances, Katherine Shear, Rachel Fox, Natalia Skritskaya, Bevin Campbell, Angela Ghesquiere, and Kim Glickman. "Catecholamine Predictors of Complicated Grief Treatment Outcomes." *International Journal of Psychophysiology* 88, no. 3 (June 2013): 349–52. https://doi.org/10.1016/j.ijpsycho.2012.09.014.

O'Connor, Mary-Frances. *The Grieving Brain: The surprising science of how we learn from love and loss*. CA: HarperCollins Publishers, 2023.

Parkes, Colin Murray. *Love and loss: The roots of grief and its complications*. London: Routledge, 2009.

Passoni, Serena, Teresa Curinga, Alessio Toraldo, Manuela Berlingeri, Isabel Fernandez, and Gabriella Bottini.
"Eye Movement Desensitization and Reprocessing Integrative Group Treatment Protocol (EMDR-
IGTP) Applied to Caregivers of Patients with Dementia." *Frontiers in Psychology* 9 (June 15, 2018).
https://doi.org/10.3389/fpsyg.2018.00967.

Prigerson, Holly G., Paul A. Boelen, Jiehui Xu, Kirsten V. Smith, and Paul K. Maciejewski. "Validation of the New
DSM-5-TR Criteria for Prolonged Grief Disorder and the PG-13-Revised (PG-13-R) Scale." *World
Psychiatry* 20, no. 1 (January 12, 2021): 96–106. https://doi.org/10.1002/wps.20823.

Rando, Therese A. *How to go on Living when someone you love dies*. Lexington, MA.: Bantam Books, 1991.

Rando, Therese A. *Treatment of Complicated Mourning*. Champaign, IL: Research Press, 1995.

Rando, Therese A., Kenneth J. Doka, Stephen Fleming, Maria Helena Franco, Elizabeth A. Lobb, Colin Murray
Parkes, and Rose Steele. "A Call to the Field: Complicated Grief in the DSM-5." *OMEGA - Journal of
Death and Dying* 65, no. 4 (December 2012): 251–55. https://doi.org/10.2190/om.65.4.a.

Shapiro, Francine. *Eye movement desensitization and reprocessing (EMDR): Basic principles, protocols, and
procedures* . 3rd ed. New York: Guilford Press, 2018.

Shapiro, Robin. *EMDR Solutions: Pathways to Healing*. New York: W.W. Norton, 2005.

Shapiro, Robin. "Visual Aids for Psychotherapy: Tools You Can Use," 2011.

Solomon, R.M., and T.A. Rando. "Treatment of Grief and Mourning through EMDR: Conceptual Considerations
and Clinical Guidelines." *European Review of Applied Psychology* 62, no. 4 (October 2012): 231–39.
https://doi.org/10.1016/j.erap.2012.09.002.

Solomon, Roger M., and Therese A. Rando. "Utilization of EMDR in the Treatment of Grief and Mourning."
*Journal of EMDR Practice and Research* 1, no. 2 (October 2007): 109–17.
https://doi.org/10.1891/1933-3196.1.2.109.

Solomon, Roger, and Barbara Hensley. "EMDR Therapy Treatment of Grief and Mourning in Times of Covid-19
(Coronavirus)." *Journal of EMDR Practice and Research* 14, no. 3 (July 29, 2020): 162–74.
https://doi.org/10.1891/emdr-d-20-00031.

Solomon, Roger, and Francine Shapiro. "EMDR and the Adaptive Information Processing Modelpotential
Mechanisms of Change." *Journal of EMDR Practice and Research* 2, no. 4 (November 2008): 315–25.
https://doi.org/10.1891/1933-3196.2.4.315.

Sprang, Ginny. "The Use of Eye Movement Desensitization and Reprocessing (EMDR) in the Treatment of Traumatic Stress and Complicated Mourning: Psychological and Behavioral Outcomes." *Research on Social Work Practice* 11, no. 3 (May 2001): 300–320. https://doi.org/10.1177/104973150101100302.

Titcombe, Lianna. "When a Beloved Pet Dies: The Best and Worst Things to Say to People in Grief." Canadian Animal Shelter & Community Medicine Association, July 21, 2022. https://www.cascma.org/when-a-beloved-pet-dies/.

Unanue, Wenceslao, Marcos Esteban Gomez Mella, Diego Alejandro Cortez, Diego Bravo, Claudio Araya-Véliz, Jesús Unanue, and Anja Van Den Broeck. "The Reciprocal Relationship between Gratitude and Life Satisfaction: Evidence from Two Longitudinal Field Studies." *Frontiers in Psychology* 10 (November 8, 2019). https://doi.org/10.3389/fpsyg.2019.02480.

"What Is Grief?" What is Grief? Accessed April 6, 2024. https://www.mayoclinic.org/patient-visitor-guide/support-groups/what-is-grief.

Walker, Matthew P. *Why we sleep: Unlocking the power of sleep and dreams.* New York, NY: Scribner, an imprint of Simon & Schuster, Inc, 2018.

Williamson, Chris. "Control Your Mind for Extreme Motivation and Focus - Andrew Huberman." YouTube, July 7, 2022. https://www.youtube.com/watch?v=31DMZLK_PPs&t=2261s.

Wojtkowiak, Joanna, Jonna Lind, and Geert Smid. "Ritual in Therapy for Prolonged Grief: A Scoping Review of Ritual Elements in Evidence-Informed Grief Interventions." *Frontiers in Psychiatry* 11 (February 3, 2021). https://doi.org/10.3389/fpsyt.2020.623835.

Wong, Joel., Jesse Owen, Nicole Gabana, Joshua Brown, Sydney McInnis, Paul Toth, and Lynn Gilman. "Does Gratitude Writing Improve the Mental Health of Psychotherapy Clients? Evidence from a Randomized Controlled Trial." *Psychotherapy Research* 28, no. 2 (May 3, 2016): 192–202. https://doi.org/10.1080/10503307.2016.1169332.

Worden, William. *Grief counselling and grief therapy: A handbook for the mental health practitioner.* 5th ed. Springer Publishing Company, LLC, 2018.